Portrait of Margaret Tate

Mistress of Montpelier, a Plantation

by

Carolyn E. Hood-Kourdache

<u>Margaret Tate</u>

By

Carolyn E. Hood-Kourdache

All rights reserved. No part of this book may be reproduced or transmitted in any form or by any means, electronic or mechanical including photocopying, recording, or by any information storage retrieval system, without the written consent of the publisher, except where permitted by law.

Printed in the U.S.A.

© *2016*

*Portrait of **Margaret Dyer-Powell Tate**, (1793-1851)
Mistress of Montpelier*

Margaret Tate

Margaret Tate

For

Hayes, Christopher, and Alex

Margaret Tate

Preface

Like many, my protracted genealogical search for unknown antecedents was prompted by a deeply felt connection to them. My journey was one of pitfalls and earthworks. I waded through fabrications mired in racial muck and gender bias, parading as truths, in Southern history.

Eventually, I encountered a nearly-nameless woman on yet another census page, "Betsy." This is my tribute to her, and so many others. "Betsy" was Grandpa John's grandmother, a Creek Indian, and David Tate's slave daughter.

> *During the Great Depression, in Baldwin County, Alabama, Grandpa John took his cattle to market. Workers corralled the animals while he customarily bargained a rate. His herd was slaughtered, prematurely, and he was offered pennies on the dollar, for the carcasses. Grandpa, bankrupted and enraged at the "joke," attacked the dealer and bit the man's ear off. A known "Indian," they let him go. His second wife, Grandma Carrie died soon after, in 1933. I never met them.*
>
> *---- Oral history*

"Betsy" was white, and quite good looking, but in the 1870 census, she was enumerated as "black."

My novitiate in genealogy was inspired by noted genealogists Gary B. Mills, acclaimed Elizabeth Shown-Mills, and Christopher Nordmann. Fortified by their work, a major family mystery was soon solved! I learned that our roots ran deep in Alabama, and that my genealogical journey was far from over.

Margaret Tate

Contents

Portrait of 1
Margaret Tate 1
Preface 6
Acknowledgments 8
Maps and Illustrations 9
Margaret Dyer-Powell 1
Known and Probable Mixed-Bloods/ 3
Choctaw Treaties During Margaret Tate's Life 5
The Patriot War of 1811-1814 12
Margaret Dyer's Lineage 15
Reuben Dyer's Land Holdings 17
David Tate's Lineage 18
Margaret's Tate's Biographical Summary 21
Excerpted from David Tate's Last Will and Testament 26
Margaret Tate's Will 35
Margaret Tate's Will, Baldwin County, Alabama, 1851 36
The Plantation 39
Josephine Bonaparte Tate Dreisbach 43
Heiress Mary Staples 45
Heiress Josephine Staples 46
Heiress Margaret [Powell] Staples 47
Heiress Mary Delphine Saunders 48
William Theophilus Powell 51
Table 1. Enumerated in Tate's Will? 57
Conclusion 58
Selected Bibliography 60

Acknowledgments

I gratefully acknowledge the many illustrations provided by the *The New York Public Library, online Digital Collections*. I wish to thank *Pam Douvier, Records Administrator for the Baldwin County Probate Judge;* and also, *Sheila B. Floyd, Baldwin County Department of Archives and History.* I gratefully acknowledge encouragement from *Jyl Hardy, former Editor, the Alabama Genealogical Society's Quarterly Magazine.* I wish to thank *Elizabeth Shown-Mills*, for her body of work. Many thanks to my family and friends, for their continuing support.

Margaret Tate

Maps and Illustrations

iv.   Frontispiece. Portrait of Mrs. Tate, circa 1819. Author's rendition.

2   *Map of Mississippi Territory in 1802. Map showing the land of the Georgia cession, Indian lands ceded to the United States in 1802. The map also includes the Mississippi Territory and Spanish West Florida. 1802-1809 Alabama Department of Archives and History. Author: Nathan H. Glick. This work is in the* **public domain** *in the United States because it was published (or registered with the U.S. Copyright Office) before January 1, 192.*

4   *Map of the Choctaw Nation in 1800. Public domain.*

6   *Portrait of Benjamin Hawkins. This work is in the public domain.*

8   *Josephine Bonaparte. This work is in the* **public domain** *in its country of origin and other countries and areas where the copyright term is the author's* **life plus 70 years or less**.

13   *"Massacre at Fort Mimms. Art and Picture Collection, The New York Public Library. "The attack on Fort Mimms." New York Public Library Digital Collections. Accessed October 17, 2015. http://digitalcollections.nypl.org/items/510d47e0-f769-a3d9-e040-e00a18064a99*

20   *Transfer of Louisiana to the United States, in 1803. Flag raising in the Place d'Armes of New Orleans, marking the transfer of*

Margaret Tate

Louisiana Purchase to the jurisdiction of the United States, December 20, 1803, as depicted by Thure de Thulstrup. Public domain.

Margaret Tate

21 *General James Wilkinson. The Miriam and Ira D. Wallach Division of Art, Prints and Photographs: Print Collection, The New York Public Library. "Jas. Wilkinson" New York Public Library Digital Collections. Accessed June 23, 2016. http://digitalcollections.nypl.org/items/510d47da-2e7d-a3d9-e040-e00a18064a99.*

26 *Aaron Burr. The Miriam and Ira D. Wallach Division of Art, Prints and Photographs: Print Collection, The New York Public Library. "Aaron Burr, Vice President of the United States, 1802." New York Public Library Digital Collections. Accessed June 23, 2016. http://digitalcollections.nypl.org/items/510d47da-2983-a3d9-e040-e00a18064a99.*

27 *"Treaty of the Hickory Ground." Art and Picture Collection, The New York Public Library. "Treaty of the Hickory Ground." New York Public Library Digital Collections. Accessed June 14, 2016. http://digitalcollections.nypl.org/items/510d47e0- f791-a3d9-e040-e00a18064a99.*

33 *Mobile Waterfront in 1830. The Miriam and Ira D. Wallach Division of Art, Prints and Photographs: Print Collection, The New York Public Library. "Mobile, Ala., the water-front." New York Public Library Digital Collections. Accessed June 23, 2016. http://digitalcollections.nypl.org/items/510d47db-1740-a3d9-e040-e00a18064a99.*

40 *Cotton gin invented in 1793. Schomburg Center for Research in Black Culture, Jean Blackwell Hutson Research and Reference Division, The New York Public Library. "The cotton gin, invented in 1793; A machine which does the work of more than 1,000 men." New York Public Library Digital Collections. Accessed June 23, 2016. http://digitalcollections.nypl.org/items/510d47df-1e06-a3d9-e040-e00a18064a99.*

Margaret Tate

54 *Shipping cotton by Torchlight on the Alabama River.* Schomburg Center for Research in Black Culture, Manuscripts, Archives and Rare Books Division, The New York Public Library. "Slaves shipping cotton by torch-light - River Alabama." New York Public Library Digital Collections. Accessed June 23, 2016. http://digitalcollections.nypl.org/items/510d47df-94c1-a3d9-e040-e00a18064a99.

Margaret Dyer-Powell

Daughter and Heir of Mary Dyer [Reuben's widow]
Widow and Relic of William Theophilus Powell, J. P.
Widow and Relic of David Tate

Margaret Tate was born Margaret Dyer, in Spanish West Florida, before 1793, to a Choctaw-metis family; died 1851, a life shared with historical icons. Just north of her family's homestead was the Creek Nation. On the West bank of the Tombigbee River, was the Choctaw Nation. Her father, wealthy Reuben Dyer, a Choctaw mixed-blood, married her mother, reputedly Mary Cussins. [Cousins] likely daughter of Richard Cussins, a British trader and Choctaw bride. Margaret Tate could read and write, but occasionally feigned illiteracy. Widowed twice, Tate sought legal counsel to settle her deceased husbands' affairs.

She was niece to Choctaw [Nancy] Haw Grey Stiggins, Joseph Stiggins' wife, and George Stiggins' mother. Relative and associate, George Stiggins, authored *Creek Indian History: A Historical Narrative of the Genealogy, Traditions, and Downfall of the Ispocoga Or Creek Indian Tribe of Indians.* Stiggins, a Natchez-Choctaw, was raised with the Creeks. So, he wrote, to some extent, about what he knew.

Mississippi Territory in 1802.

Margaret Dyer, daughter of privilege, groomed to marry wealth, chose wealthy William Theophilus Powell, justice of the peace, and cousin of Osceola [William "Billy" Powell], a Creek Indian. Their children were Mary Delphine, b. 1810, William Theophilus, b. 1817 and Martha. Her household was populated with slaves. Margaret Dyer-Powell's associates were many Choctaw metis, and included George Stiggins, Penny Coleman, Mary Randon, and other acculturated mixed-blood Indians. The Five Civilized Tribes were one people.

Known and Probable Mixed-Bloods/
Choctaw metis surnames[1]

Adcock

Bailey

Brown

Bryant

Coleman

Cousins

Dale

Durant

Dyer

Fletcher

Hall

Harris

Hollinger

Holmes

Juzan

Kennedy

Le Flore

McGee

McIntosh

Parson

Shaw

Stiggins

Vaughn

Williams

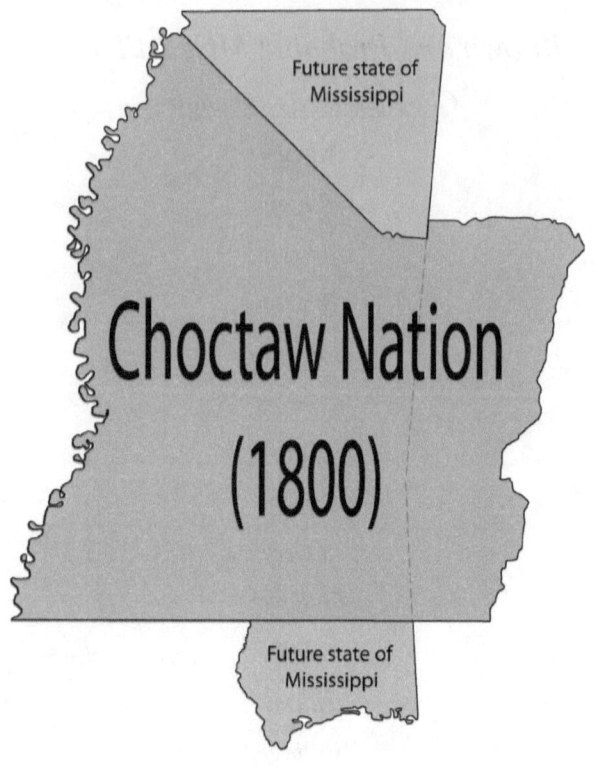

Individual Choctaw mixed-bloods reliably negotiated one-sided treaties erasing collective Choctaw proprietorship over their primordial lands. Millions of acres were ceded in exchange for Arkansas territory (already occupied by settlers), to the detriment of the Choctaw Nation. Mixed-bloods received land reservations and stipends that did not, nor could not compensate the Choctaw at large. The following treaties evince the wholesale abandonment of Mississippi Territory (the Choctaw Nation) by its leaders - generally the wealthiest among them to the expanding United States.

Choctaw Treaties During Margaret Tate's Life[2]

Treaty of Fort Adams, 1801, United States Mississippi Territory Re-defined Choctaw cession to England and permission for Natchez Trace 2,641,920 acres (10,691.5 km2)

Treaty of Hoe Buckintoopa, 1803, United States Choctaw Nation Small cession of Tombigbee River and redefined English treaty of 1765 853,760 acres (3,455.0 km2)

Mount Dexter, 1805, United States Choctaw Nation (Mississippi) Large cession from Natchez District to the Tombigbee Alabama River watershed 4,142,720 acres (16,765.0 km2)

Treaty of Fort St. Stephens, 1816, United States Fort St. Stephens (Alabama) Ceded all Choctaw land east of Tombigbee River 10,000 acres (40 km2) Treaty of Mount Dexter 1805 United States Choctaw Nation (Mississippi) Large cession from Natchez District to the Tombigbee Alabama River watershed 4,142,720 acres (16,765.0 km2)

Treaty of Doak's Stand, 1820, United States Natchez Trace, Choctaw Nation (Mississippi) Exchanged cession in Mississippi for parcel in Arkansas and prepare the Choctaws to become citizens of the United States 5,169,788 acres (20,921.39 km2)

The final straw:

Treaty of Dancing Rabbit Creek, 1830, United States Choctaw Nation (Mississippi) Removal and granting U.S. citizenship 10,523,130 acres (42,585.6 km2)

Benjamin Hawkins, Commissioner Plenipoteniary of the United States, from North Carolina, was usually present in the Jefferson scheme to denude the Indian Nations. His was first among the signatures for the above-referenced "treaties."

Slaveholder Margaret Dyer-Powell Tate, naturally agreed with the privileged. It was in the best interests of landowners to stock their property with slaves. Spain and France held dominion; and must be expelled from the continent, in order to further the scheme of transgenerational slavery, without taxation. Aggrandizement was a religion. Exploitation of the lesser was the framework. Aaron Burr was initially welcomed before he was arrested. He wined and dined with the Powells, Bates, and Rains, at Tensaw. Their leanings were similar to those of conservative Mexicans, under Santa Ana.

During this period of intrigue and war, settlers in the Tensaw/Tombigbee region considered themselves patriots. They cheered when Georgians invaded East Florida in 1812, and seized territory on the Southern border. In effect, this was an assault against Spain, and her version of slavery. Those same usurpers sought to retrieve their property, runaway slaves, to prevent Spain from readily recruiting blacks, for her army against them.

Likewise, Tensaw settlers welcomed the capture of Mobile by

General James Wilkinson, in 1813. Wilkinson was a surreptitiously paid Spanish agent. To insist that the Red Stick War of the Creek Nation was ignited by renegade Little Warrior; or the fatal attack against Mims' fortifications, is to obviate the truth. Americans had clandestinely waged war against Spain, since Aaron Burr's intrigues of 1803, allegedly to free Texas.

Josephine Bonaparte

Incessant pressures were applied to the Creek and Chocktaw Nations to cede more territory, years prior to the onset of the world War of 1812. Margaret and David Tate, later expressed their admiration for Napoleon by christening their only daughter for the beautiful, vivacious, and deceased, Josephine Bonaparte.

After the death of her first husband, William Theophilus Powell, circa 1817, in the first Seminole War, Powell married (cohabited with) David Tate, remnant chief of the Creek Nation, by 1819. He was the widowed husband of her niece, Mary Louise Randon. Dyer-Powell's sister, Tura Dyer was the concubine, or second wife to John Randon, and died with him at Fort Mims.

Fort Mims was the scene of a successful slave revolt on American soil. Seven hundred slaves of Indian descent joined with an equal number of dissident Red Stick warriors to wipe out the inhabitants of Samuel Mims fortified plantation. Much has been made of the "massacre." No record, however, mentions the disappearance of the hundreds of slaves that escaped August 30, 1813.[3]

The settlers had no chance at Fort Mims. According to Swan's drawings of the encampment, both the east and west gates were open before the attack. The slaves were outside the fort, and spoke Muscogee. They themselves were Creek. Therefore, it is reasonable to conclude that the attack was a slave revolt.

Margaret's mother, Mary [Cussins] Dyer died at Fort Mims, as the claimant, Theophilus Powell, swore:

> ... *I do solemnly swear that the above is a true acct. of property taken or destroyed by the Indians subsequent to the attack on Fort Mims belonging to the estate of Mary Dyer of which I am the administrator, as I verily believe.   - Thelps Powell*[4]

Dyer-Powell suffered the loss of friends and family, alongside her sister, Tura Dyer-Randon, and mother Mary Dyer. Dyer-Powell made a wartime claim on behalf of her father (he predeceased any hostilities). A claim for her father on behalf of her mother, was the basis of Dyer's claim. A claim for her father had greater weight. His earlier death was a factual inconvenience. Reuben held numerous properties, one of which was mentioned in the following claim, in Louisiana, in 1820:

> *State of Louisiana, Parish of Feliciana:*
>
> *Before me, William C. Wade, judge of the parish, aforesaid, came and appeared James Thomas, who, being duly sworn, says that a grant or ricket, calling for the Bayou Boeuf, adjoining lands claimed by Reuben Dyer, was placed in deponent's hands to send on to Judge Henry Johnson, a member of Congress, by a legal representative of William Collins ...*[5]

Dyer-Powell was only 26, when she attached herself to David Tate. Technically a Creek chieftain, his appearance, and demeanor belied his bloodline. His wealth and good looks made up for any character flaws. Tate was a fit match for Dyer-Powell. Their union ensured uninterrupted status of comfort built on white privilege and black slavery. After only 10 years of marriage, Tate succumbed to illness, and died. His legacy was the manumission of his slaves, and the persistent struggle to retain his land holdings, appropriated by the United States, at the Treaty of Fort Jackson, in 1814.

Of course, on marrying David Tate, Margaret Dyer-Powell became the sister-in-law of the infamous William Weatherford. The so-called "Red Eagle," leader of the Red Stick warriors that perpetrated the massacre, at Fort Mims. Weatherford died in 1824. Tate died in 1829. His plantation was styled "Montpelier," in homage to Secretary Henry Knox' home, styled similarly, in Vermont.

Tate's only child with Dyer-Powell, Josephine Bonaparte Tate, married James Denny Dreisbach in 1844. Margaret Tate was the guardian of her daughter's financial holdings.[6] Margaret Tate could actually conduct business, and confidently sign her name. She was a literate woman in a time of predominant illiteracy for both sexes.

Margaret Tate died in 1851. In her Will, she bequeathed 54 people to her family. Within her household, resided her deceased husband's children, by her rivals, his enslaved wives. Margaret Tate disposed of them. Within a year of her death, Tate's only son, William Theophilus Powell, died. Josephine and her husband, an attorney immediately commenced litigation against Tate's estate, as well as William Powell in search of her father's legacy. They failed to uncover any substantial wealth. Her mother and possibly her brother had disposed of or exhausted any cash holdings, and had sold or freed 100 "slaves." Also, eleven girls were unaccounted for at the conclusion of the lawsuit. Possibly, they were the same "little negroes" [children] educated alongside Josephine, at the Suggsville Institute; [her sisters], the children of David Tate.

After the Removal of 1830, Alabama adopted stringent legislation regarding slaves. Manumitted slaves were forced to leave the state. Creeks adopted transgenerational slavery, in 1818. Simultaneously, Native Americans were less tolerated in their own land. "Removal!" was the cry of the day, and government policy.

Earlier, in 1811, through 1814, conflict swirled throughout the region. Besides the decimation of the Choctaw Nation via treaty, American settlers, by hook or by crook sought unencumbered expansion, as promised by their elected officials. Designs upon East and West Florida were implemented by force. Georgians invaded East Florida, in what is euphemistically referred to as the Patriots' War.

The Patriot War of 1811-1814

> *An armed force of over one hundred and fifty Georgians invaded East Florida, calling themselves "Patriots." They took a small Spanish post north of St. Augustine. Implying that they were Floridians, they offered the area of their conquest to the United States as new territory. President Madison had sent an accredited representative, General George Matthews from Georgia, who accepted the conquest on behalf of the United States. As this force moved to take control of St. Augustine, some English-speaking residents of the province manifested support for the American Patriots, including the wealthy planter Zephaniah Kingsley. Others did not and the Patriots found that their invasion did not motivate a successful uprising of the province's populace against the Spanish authorities. The Patriots eventually failed to take St. Augustine successfully and, once the War of 1812 began, the Madison administration withdrew its tacit support of the Patriots; Madison did not want Spain to ally with Great Britain in the larger conflict because of events in East Florida.* [7]

Under Spanish law, slaves enjoyed a more humane existence. They were able to obtain their freedom, on the payment plan; could testify in courts regarding their treatment by sadistic slaveholders; openly practice their religion, be baptized; and avoid transgenerational servitude. In short, their status, under Spanish dominion, was a flagrant threat to slavery suffered in neighboring American (United States) territory. Runaway slaves flocked by the thousands to St.

Augustine, Florida. Black men readily enlisted in British and Spanish armed forces.

Daughter and Heir of Reuben Dyer

Reuben Dyer died before the events of August 30, 1813. In fact, he was not enumerated in the 1810 Mississippi Territorial Census. His widow, Mary Dyer, on the other hand, was killed at Fort Mims. Her son-in-law, Theophilus Powell, represented her estate, as reported in Lackey's *Frontier Claims in the Lower South*.

Massacre at Fort Mimms, 1813. Courtesy of the New York Public Library, Digital Collections.

Margaret Dyer's Lineage

```
Dyer = Choctaw maiden      Richard Cussins [Cousins] = Choctaw
                                         maiden
         |                                   |
              Reuben Dyer = Mary Cussins
                         |
   _____|_____
   |                          |                           |
Margaret Dyer         Martha [Polly] Dyer            Tura Dyer
= 1. William Theophilus Powell    = John             = John
   _____|_____  Weatherford        Randon
   |              |              |
Mary D.        Wm. Th. Jr.    Martha
= David        = Mary         = Jason
Moniac         Bryant         Staples

= 2. David Tate
       |
Josephine Bonaparte Tate
= James Denny Dreisbach
```

William Powell [I] = 1. Elizabeth [Isabel Nash]
                      = 2. African or Indian
                        maiden
___1785 McIntosh's Bluff [Spanish Land Grant]___

| | | | | | | |
Martha Joyce   Elijah   Thomas John   James   **William T. [II]**
  =   =   =   d. August
1816   John Johnston   Genoveva Dolives   = Margaret
Dyer

William Theophilus Powell, [III], Mary Delphine,   Margaret
= Martha Ann Bryant [Crow]   = D. Moniac   = J. Staples

  | | |
Robert   Fredonia   Marsalina[8]

Reuben Dyer = Mary Cussins

  | | |
Margaret   Tura   Martha "Polly"
  =   =   =   =
1. Wm. T. Powell   John Randon   John Weatherford
  =
  |
Wm. T. Powell [III]
= 2. David Tate

Reuben Dyer's Land Holdings
and Close Relatives (Richard Coleman and Joseph Stiggins)

From: *Grassroots of America*   Volume: Page

Dyer Revben   1:832
Dyer, Reuben   1:630, 643, 818, 819, 820, 822, 828, 850; **4:502, 503**

Volume I: Index Page 829

Dyer, Reuben **578**, 590 **[591], 740, 767**

1.   640 acres, Margin of the Tensaw River, Spanish occupancy, October 22, 1797; 640 acres Tensaw River, Spanish occupancy, 1797; "this claim is supported agreeably to the requirements of law. . ."

> ***Reuben Dyer's Case No. 222*** *on the docket of the Board, and No. 46 on the books of the Register, Claim: A donation of six hundred and forty acres, under the second section of the act.*
> *The claimant presented his claim together with a surveyor's plot, in the following words and figures, viz.:*
>
> *To the Commissioners appointed in pursuance of the act of Congress, passed 3d March, 1803, for receiving and adjusting the claims to lands south of Tennessee, and east of Pearl river. . . .*
>
> *Joseph Stiggins and Reuben Dyer* . .
>
> **Case No. 223 - Richard Coleman**
> *Joseph Stiggins for Richard Coleman*

Case No. 224 - Joseph Stiggins

David Tate's Lineage

Sehoy I = 1a. Creek Chief Red Shoes I
|
Red Shoes II
= 2a. allegedly Louis Marchand de Cortel[9]

Sehoy II = 1b. Tuckabatchee Creek Chief

= 2b. Malcolm McPherson, Scots trader, L. McGillivray associate

Sehoy III McPherson (Creek metis)   Chief Malcolm McPherson of
    = 1c. William Dixon Moniac   [Tallasee] Hickory Ground[10]
    = 2c. Col. David Tait
                                           = 3b. Lachlin McGillivray

David Tate, et al.
= 3c. Charles Weatherford   Alexander   Sophia   Jeanette
        | = **Elise Moniac** = Ben Durant = Milfort
William Weatherford, et al.
                                             Elizabeth, et al   Latchlin
al.   Durant, et
                                                             = Capt. Isaacs aka
                                                             Nomathle Emautla[11] [12]

                       David Tate =   **Flora**[13]

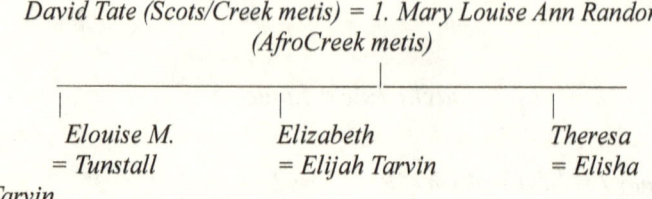

4. Tate's daughter, *Elouise [Eloisa] Tunstall*, wife of Tunstall, received an unspecified portion of her father's estate, in the Nuncupative Will.

5. Daughter, *Elizabeth [Elijah] Tarvin*, received four or five slaves and an unspecified portion of her father's estate, in the Nuncupative Will.

6. Daughter, *Theresa [Elisha] Tarvin*, received an unspecified portion of her father's estate, in the Nuncupative Will.

7. *Widow Margaret Tate* received the bulk of her husband's estate.

8. Daughter, minor, *Josephine Tate* received two fillies, and little else of her father's estate, in the Nuncupative Will.

*David Tate (Scots/Creek metis) = 1. Mary Louise Ann Randon
(AfroCreek metis)*

= 2. Margaret Dyer-Powell
|
Josephine Bonaparte Tate [Dreisbach]

Margaret's Tate's Biographical Summary

1793 Born in Spanish West Florida (probably earlier).
1793 *Eli Whitney invented the cotton gin*

1800 *Married William Theophilus Powell*
1801 *Treaty of Fort Adams- permission for Natchez trace*
1803 *Treaty of Buckintoopa, cession of Tombigbee River*
1803 *Louisiana Purchase*

Transfer of Louisiana - Purchase in 1803.

1805 *Creek land cession to Georgia Treaty of Mount Dexter, Choctaw cession*

1810 Father Reuben Dyer presumably died before Census taken.
Annexation of West Florida attempt.
1811 Mobile captured General James Wilkinson.

Gen. Wilkinson

1811-
1814 The Patriot War of East Florida.

Tecumseh pleads his case against neutrality.

July
1813 Burnt Corn Creek skirmishes, failures, Death of Tecumseh.

August
1813 Fort Mims "Massacre"

1816 Treaty of Fort St. Stephens, ceded all Choctaw land east of Tombigbee River

July
1817 Indemnity for Damages by Creek Indians Awarded and paid for Creek War Claims

Received

1819 *circa "Married"* **David Tate**
1820 *Treaty of Doak's Stand, Choctaw Nation (Mississippi) exchanged cession in Mississippi for parcel in Arkansas - U.S. citizenship*

March
1825 *Act of Congress of, land allotment secured*

March

1829 *Husband, David Tate died at Montpelier Death Bed Wish to Free His Slaves*

1830 *Choctaw Treaty of Dancing Rabbit Rock*

Patrick Byrne, Judge CCBC

An inventory and appraisement of the following property found among the estate of David Tate and which was in his possession at his death but which the administrators claim to be the property of the estate of Theophilus Powel [sic] and which the deceased never did claim the right of and which the administrators submit for appraisement so that if the right should have been in D. Tate, Justice may be done.

* * * * * * *

Negroes belonging to the estate of Theophilus Powel :

Anderson	*125.00*
Melissa	*175.00*
Old Peg	*.125*
Hannah	*250.00*
Clarinder	*200.00*
Allick	*150.00*
Abbey	*115.00*
Cuff	*110.00*
Sylvia	*100.00*
Amy	**400.00**
Winney	*250.00*
Nancy [sic]	*300.00*
Little Ned	*400.00*
Deana [sic]	**100.00**
Sambo [sic]	*225.00*
Peg and Child Ben	*400.00*
Jordan	*100.00*
Sarah	*125.00*
Old Harry	*250.00*
1 old gray Horse	*20.00*
	$38,415.125

Excerpted from David Tate's Last Will and Testament

...

Josephine and her son, William, all and all manner of claim to the real or personal estate and the increase of the same which was of the late Theophilus Powell for which the said David Tate deceased in any way received with his wife Margaret, or in any way acquired in her right

and and [sic] Covenant and agree the same shall be separate by the administrators with the Will annexed and surrendered to the said Margaret, and her children never to be claimed by us,

that Margaret Tate widow shall have in her own right forever as apart or the whole as the case may be of her share of the slaves of the said David Tate, the following Negroes to wit: **Jonah**, **Flora**, **Hardy, Phoebe** *and her child,* **Bella, William** *the blacksmith and his wife Daphne and their children, Louise, and Harry,* **Maria, Cuff**, *Old Joe and* **Sickey**,

and that Josephine Tate shall have in her own right forever as the whole or part or as the case may be of her share of the slaves of the estate of her father, David Tate the following slaves to wit: Sharper and his wife Abby and their child George, London and his wife Esther and their son, Jonah, Ned and his wife, Charlotte and their boy Ogesas, [Oscar] Stephen, Jimbo and his wife, Rose and their children, Bill, Patty, Daniel and Milly and a Young fellow called Daniel, Ben and his wife Bet,

...

The parties agree the residence of the estate of the said David Tate after the separation of the Dyer, Powell, and Randon estates as before named shall be divided in five equal shares unto Elouisa Tunstall, and heirs, one other to Betsy Tarvin and heirs, one other to Teresa Tarvin and heirs, one other to Josephine Tate and the other to Margaret Tate the widow and relic.

The Negroes before mentioned as the part of Margaret and Josephine as many as may be living to constitute a part or the whole as the case may be of their respective dividends of said estate,

. . . 2nd of February, 1830. In witness whereof the parties have hereunto set their hands and seals.

In presence of
    Margaret Tate $_{her\,X\,mark}$ *{rubric seal}*
Mother and Guardian {rubric seal}
    Enoch Parsons
    Josephine Tate by M. Tate
    James Dillett

. . .

Dyer was natural heir to Reuben [Nathan] Dyer, Choctaw metis, and Mary Cussins [Cousins]. Relative, George Stiggins[14] and William Brown were her securities, during administration of her first husband's Estate, in 1816. In 1832, Joseph Booth, Thomas Atkinson, and Lee Slaughter were her securities in the administration of the Guardianship over her daughter, minor, Josephine Tate.

It was during that Guardianship that Margaret Tate's literacy was revealed. She actually signed receipts for payments made on behalf of her daughter's estate. And, in so doing was responsible for any pilferage or incompetence that occurred.

On January 2, 1817, Margaret Powell petitioned the U.S. House of Representatives for relief for her family's losses during the Creek War. Other parties to the petition were: her sister, Patsy [Martha] Dyer [Weatherford], Arthur Sizemore, Mary Sizemore, and Peggy Bailey.[15] Her older sister, Tura Elizabeth Dyer [Randon], second wife to John Randon, died with him at Fort Mims.

Theophilus Powell, Justice of the Peace,[16] left Dyer-Powell with three children, and a sizable estate. Theophilus Powell was the son of William Powell, an original settler of McIntosh Bluff, Mississippi Territory. William Powell obtained a Spanish land grant, in 1787. Powell's sister-in-law was Martha Bates, and her brother-in-law was Cornelius Rains of the famous Aaron Burr arrest, in 1807.

Aaron Burr.
Courtesy of the New York Public Library, Digital Collections.

On May 14, 1812, West Florida was annexed as Mississippi Territory; and 1812 - 1817 was the Mississippi Territorial Period. June, 1812, was the commencement of the War of 1812. The war of aggression of 1813, against the Creek Nation, has been mischaracterized as a civil war. The Nation wasn't exactly divided, rather there was dissension in the rank and file of Creek citizenry. There was no civil war, only 160 sellouts fighting with Jackson versus thousands of nativist warriors. It devolved into a war of extermination, namely the Red Stick War of 1813 - 1814. Margaret Dyer-Powell would lose most of her family, but retain her wealth.

After the customary three-year mourning period, Dyer-Powell married John Randon's son-in-law, David Tate. No record of nuptials was uncovered. Margaret Dyer, the wealthiest woman in Alabama Territory, with substantial land holdings, wielded the power to choose. And, she chose David Tate.

*Treaty of the Hickory Ground.
Courtesy of the New York Public
Library, Digital collections.*

At cessation of hostilities, the Creeks were decimated by Jackson. Elite "friendly Indians," received land reservations, as their indemnification for losses sustained. Typically, women received nothing for their losses. Reuben Dyer's death was reported as a war event. Dyer predeceased 1813, and was not an actual victim of Indian warfare. Mary Dyer, his widow was enumerated in the 1810 Census for Baldwin County, without Reuben. In her household were two white males under 21, two white females under 21, two white females over 21, and 12 slaves.[17] Reuben Dyer was not enumerated in his second wife, Maria Josephina Juzan aka Mary Hollinger's household either. Mary and Margaret were Mary Dyer's heirs; her other children were deceased. Reuben Dyer predeceased the Act of Congress, of 1817, as Margaret Dyer-Powell, heir of Mary Dyer, widow of Reuben Dyer received a share in a land reserve,

> "*in pursuance of an Act of Congress, passed on the 3d of March 1817 entitled 'an Act making provision for the location of the Lands reserved by the first Article of the Treaty of the 9th of August, 1814, between the United States and the Creek Nation . . .'"*[18]

During the attack on Fort Mims, Margaret Dyer-Powell was at Mobile, at Fort Charlotte with her younger sister and ward, Martha "Polly" Dyer, the future Mrs. John Weatherford. Her first husband, Theophilus Powell sold slaves that belonged to her, to General Jackson:

> *In September, Theophilus Powell sold Jackson five slaves--**Seller, Jack, Hannah, Sam and Amey**--whom he claimed "by virtue of his intermarriage with one of the daughters and legal heirs of Wm. [Reuben] Dyer who was killed at the siege and destruction of Fort Mims."*[19]

Powell's three children and heirs were Mary Delphine, Martha, and William Theophilus Powell.[20] Dyer and David Tate had only one child together, Josephine Bonaparte Tate [James D. Dreisbach]. Although Choctaw metis, Dyer responded to interrogatories at the *Weatherford v. Weatherford, et al. trial*, that she did not speak the Creek language, nor was she familiar with Creek lore and culture relating to marriage.[21] Considering that she was Choctaw and not Creek, her responses were plausibly truthful. However, when we consider her treatment of Flora, we note that she was disingenuous.

According to Stiggins, it was customary for Creek men to marry the female relative of their deceased wife. Tate legally married Penny Coleman, another EuroIndian, in June of 1814, at Mobile, within a year of the violent death of his first wife Mary Louise Randon at Fort Mims. Tate and Powell were neighbors and socially acquainted, but she evidently did not spark his attentions until well after the death of Coleman in 1817, and the purchase of his concubine, "Flora," in 1819. Many Indian countrymen maintained multiple households.

David Tate (Scots/Creek metis) = *1. Mary Louise Ann Randon*
(AfroCreek metis)

Elouise M.	*Elizabeth*	*Theresa*
= Tunstall Tarvin	*= Elijah Tarvin*	*= Elisha*

2. Penny Coleman
3. Margaret Dyer-Powell

Josephine Tate Dreisbach

4. "Flora" McGillivray

Susan James **Stratford Monday**	*Lucinda Thomas*	*Bella Harris*	**Betsy**

5. Mary [Mariah] Tate

Todd [Thaddeus] Tate

6. Amy Webster

| *Fanny* | *Milly* | *Tena* | **[Delia]** |

42

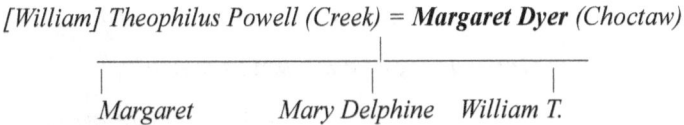

[William] Theophilus Powell (Creek) = **Margaret Dyer** *(Choctaw)*

Margaret   Mary Delphine   William T.

The following relationships existed based on the above-delineated bloodlines:

    1.   David Tate was John Randon's son-in-law;

    4.   Adam Hollinger was the son-in-law of Pierre Juzan;[22] [23]

    5.   John Randon, David Tate's father-in-law was the brother-in-law of Margaret Dyer-Powell;

    6.   David Tate's first wife, Mary Louise Randon was the niece of his third wife Margaret Dyer. Tura Elizabeth Dyer was John Randon's second wife or concubine, which made Margaret Dyer-Powell, Mary Randon's aunt.

    7.   Dyer and Tate were long acquainted;

    8.   John Randon was Thomas G. Holmes' son-in-law.

David Tate's first and second marriages were recorded.[24]

Once again, Powell, as was customary, shared her husband with a slave concubine. "Amy," was too young to have been the concubine of slaveholder, Theophilus Powell. David Tate was available. Amy, remembered as a true beauty, had many children. Powell was 15 years Tate's junior. In David Tate's Will, he endeavored to free his children, namely, Wallace, Todd [Thaddeus], and others. However, his widow and relic, Margaret Tate saw things differently, and omitted references to manumission in his proven Will, or the Final Settlement for his estate. Thus, Powell denied recorded freedom to her husband's children and slaves.[25] Margaret Tate was remembered as vicious and vindictive, severing three fingers from "Amy's" hands because she could read, after the death of her husband.[26] Was the creature that condemned Amy to "cropped" hands, Margaret Tate -- the same benevolent woman that provided for the education of nine to 11 "little negroes," with her own daughter, between 1832 and 1834; at the Suggsville Institute?[27]

> *"Heav'n has no rage like love to hatred turn'd*
> **Nor Hell a fury, like a woman scorn'd."**
>
> --- William Congreve
>
> *English playwright and poet*

Margaret Tate's cousin, George Stiggins, suffered as many other remnant Indians, especially after Removal. Their land reservations were of little use, surrounded by hostile whites. Stiggins, frustrated with discrimination and limited opportunities for his children, petitioned the federal government for a waiver to sell his property:

> *named individuals . . . state that they are dissatisfied with their residence among the whites, by whom they are viewed as inferiors, and treated with contempt and contumely; that they are desirous to remove beyond the Mississippi, and reside among their brethren and equals. . . cannot do so without incurring a forfeiture . . . George Stiggins states, in substance, that he holds a like reservation, under the treaty made with the Creek Indians, at Fort Jackson, on the 9th of August, 1814; that he has a family of children, that he is desirous to rear and educate, but he is poor and without the means to do so, unless the United States will make a like relinquishment and enable him to sell.. . . Under the treaty with the Creek Indians a forfeiture would occur by the removal of the reservee or his descendants.*[28]

The one-drop rule was of little use to those mixed-bloods having one white ancestor. Their skin color belied their "whiteness." They failed to convince whites of their racial equality, at a time of growing white supremacy.

Margaret Tate's Will
Baldwin County, Alabama, 1851[29]

Mobile Waterfront, 1830

Transcribed are the pertinent facts as excerpted from Margaret Tate's Will (Tate's Will). Further, usage of the term "negro," is a direct transcription from an historical document, and in no way reflective of contemporary bias, but rather the penman of the time. To be a "negro," was to be defined as a slave. There were persons in the below enumeration that were in fact not slaves nor negroes. The same caveat would apply to "boy" and "girl." Persons of color, especially slaves, no matter their age, were not accorded the same deference enjoyed today. The enumeration:

Margaret Tate's Will, Baldwin County, Alabama, 1851[30]

[headers added]

Name	Gender	Heir
		to my beloved daughter Mary Delphine Saunders
Sam	one negro man	[David Moniac's widow married Thomas Saunders; testified in case of Weatherford v. Weatherford, et al.]
Mariah	one negro woman	
Amy	one negro girl	
Sam	one negro boy	
Daniel	one negro boy	
Peggy	one negro girl	
Harry	one negro boy	
		beloved daughter Margaret Staples and her heirs
Job	one negro man	
Silva	one negro girl and child	
Betsy	**one negro woman and her child named Jonas [John or Jack]**	
Sandy	one negro boy	
Twine	one negro boy	
Tobe	one negro boy	
Malissa	one negro girl and her two children	
Ned	one negro man	
Harry	one negro boy	
Patience	one negro girl	
		children of beloved son, William T.

Powell
William one negro man
Aaron one negro man
Cuff one negro man
Stephen one negro boy
Elouisa one negro woman
Siky   and her four children
Daphney
Chloe
Tab
Poss   one negro woman

beloved daughter
Josephine Bonaparte Tate
[James D. Dreisback]

Dick   one negro man
Bella   one negro woman
*   and her four children*
Pheabe
Hardy
Dick
Mary
Harry one negro boy
Lige   one negro boy
Rose   one negro girl
Amy   one negro woman
*   and her three children*
Tena
Milly
Fanny
Flora   one negro woman
Jonah one old negro man   ... wish the old negro man
named Jonah shall do

no hard work

beloved Grand daughter
Mary Staples

Clander   one negro woman
*   and three of her children*

Alec
Philip
Dilsy

beloved Grand daughter
Josephine Staples

Or   one negro boy

It is my request that Hardy and his wife, Pheobe shall be set at liberty. I do not wish them to be slaves after my death. It is my wish that my old negro woman Siky shall remain with my daughter Josephine during her life.

Witnesses:
J. W. Shomo   [sister-in-law, Rosanna's husband]
             her
Margaret   X$_{mark}$ Tate
J.[ohn] D. Weatherford [brother-in-law]

Admitted to Probate 27th March A.D. 1851
Patrick Byrne, Judge

The Plantation

M o n t p e l i e r

<u>Mount Pleasant, Monroe County</u>

"the lowest condition in life, with freedom attending it, is better than the most exalted station under the restricts of slavery."
-- Samuel Burris, The Liberator

David Tate's youngest daughter, Josephine [Tate] Dreisbach and her attorney husband, James D. Dreisbach brought suit against Margaret Tate's estate and that of her son, William Powell. Dreisbach sought to liquidate his wife's fortune. David Tate's estate was appraised at $48,000.00, in 1829. Josephine was a paper heiress. Their efforts were far from expectations, as her mother squandered the wealth, and freed 100 slaves.

The return address for the Dreisbachs, in 1852, was [Montpelier] Mount Pleasant, Monroe County. They had apparently taken up residence with her mother, prior to 1850. The Staples (daughter Margaret and Jason), lived at Beat 1, Monroe County, in 1870. However, still no record was found to indicate that the "place," was anything more than a large farm, without evincing plantation domicile, or extant slave quarters, iconic of grandiose Southern plantations.

Margaret Tate's Will described the location of her prime real estate as excerpted:[31]

> *My plantation situated and described as follows: The South East fraction quarter of section nineteen, in Township four of range three east, containing one Hundred & fifty acres and sixty five hundredths of an acre. The west half of the north west quarter of section nineteen, in township four range three east, containing eighty acres. The east subdivision of the west fraction of the north half, west of the Alabama River of section nineteen in Township four, of range three east containing one hundred and fifty two acres ...*

The above description coincides with that provided by the Bureau of Land Management.[32] The second sentence above began the desciption of land owned by David Tate's nephew and heir, David Moniac:

> *NOW KNOW YE, That the UNITED STATES OF AMERICA, in consideration of the premises, and in conformity with the several acts of Congress, in such case made and provided, have given and granted, and, by these presents, do give and grant, unto the said David Moniac, and to his heirs, the said tract, above described ... Andrew Jackson . . . 1833*[33]

A complete explanation is also provided here for geographical context and understanding of how to read these land extracts.[34]

> *Margaret Tate - Certificate No. 4034*
>
> *...the South East fractional quarter of Section Nineteen, in Township Four, of Range Three East, in the district of lands - subject to sale at St. Stephens, Alabama. Containing One hundred and fifty eight acres, and sixty five hundredths of an acre,...*

30 May 1833

Additional properties were found to be relevant.[35] Margaret Tate - Certificate No. 2782, and Margaret Tate - Certificate No. 7743.

Three counties in Alabama, Baldwin, Clarke, and Monroe, come together and overlap, in what must have been part of the Tate Plantation. If you like to walk, you can imagine walking in a straight line for 36 miles due east, marking your distance every six miles as Range 1, Range 2, Range 3, and so on. Once you have completed your 36 miles, you will then turn and head due south for another 36 miles, marking your six mile increments, your Township markings, as you go, until you have marked the perimeter of 36 square miles. This area might represent Township 4. You may proceed until you have marked four distinct townships, and imagine that you are standing where former slaves stood. Make sure that you start in the northern section of Baldwin County so that you will be sure to touch either Clarke or Monroe or both Counties. Now you will have a feel for the location of the former landscape.

Of course, if you want the exact location, you are welcome to visit the Bureau of Land Management. There you may perform a search with the exact coordinates for Tate's Will, and thus, locate Township 1-4, etc. It's just not as much fun.

The University of Georgia's site, has an exquisite explanation of the Survey for the United States, created in my home State of Ohio. Maps of Baldwin and neighboring Clarke and Monroe Counties are presented for clarification.

The Cotton Gin, Invented in 1793.

Josephine Bonaparte Tate Dreisbach
Daughter and Heir of
David Tate and Margaret Dyer-Powell
1827 - 1908

Margaret Tate's youngest daughter, Josephine Bonaparte Tate, born 1827, Little River, Alabama, married Major James Denny Dreisbach, resided in Baldwin County, died 1908, Baldwin County.[36] Some of her children were: Percy, Clara, Josephine, Sehoy Rosa, Lee, Bertha, and Annie.[37] Josephine was neighbor to her half-brother and nephew, Thaddeus Tate, and his son, Henry Tate.[38]

1860[39]

Baldwin County, Alabama

James D. Dresback [Driesbach] = Josephine B. [Tate] Dreisbach

	44	
32		

| Ida T. | Tait R. | | C. H. | Percy W. | Mabel |
| F.A. | A. C. | Kate | | | |

1870[40]
Baldwin County, Alabama

James D. Dresback [Driesbach] = Josephine B. [Tate] Dreisbach

Ida	Florence	Charles H.	Percy W. Mabel
Arthur C.	Maude		
	Lee	Bertha	Clara

1880

Baldwin County, Alabama

James D. Dresback [Driesbach] = Josephine B. [Tate] Dreisbach

Percy W	Clara	Josephine	Sehoy R.
Lee	Bertha	Annie	

Heiress Mary Staples

Margaret Tate's granddaughter, Mary J. Staples, born August 1, 1833, at Little River, Baldwin County, Alabama, never married, died July 18, 1922, at Little River.[41]

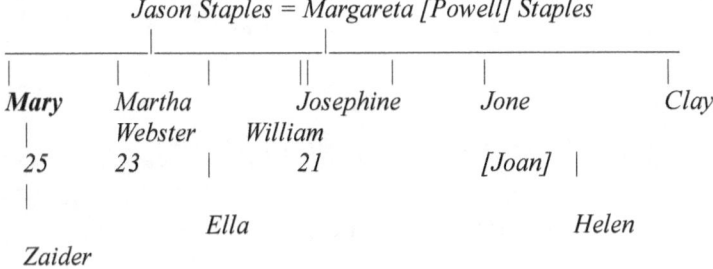

1860

Monroe County, Alabama[42]

```
            Jason Staples = Margareta [Powell] Staples
     |        |         |      ||       |        |          |
   Mary     Martha           Josephine  Jone              Clay
    |       Webster   William    21     [Joan]    |
    25        23         |                        |
    |                   Ella                    Helen
  Zaider
```

Staples resided at Beat 1, Monroe County, for the 1870 enumeration, with her family.[43] Her siblings were Henry C., Daniel, William, Catherine, Ellen and Yodell.[44] Henry Clay, Helen [Ellen] and William still resided with their mother, in 1880, but in Montgomery Hill, Baldwin County.[45] Mary Staples was enumerated with her brother Henry Clay Staples for the 1900, 1910, and 1920 Census, for Baldwin County. Their immediate neighbors were James D. Dreisbach and Charles Dreisbach, his son.

Heiress Josephine Staples

Margaret Tate's granddaughter, Josephine Staples, born circa 1839, at Little River, Baldwin County, Alabama, never married, died unknown, was deeded only one person, "Or [Orne Harper]."

Heiress Josephine Staples

1860

Monroe County, Alabama[46]

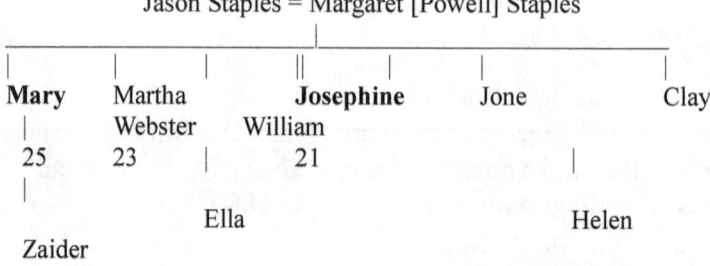

Heiress Margaret [Powell] Staples

Margaret Tate's daughter by William Theophilus Powell, Margaret Powell Staples, born circa 1817, in Alabama,[47] married Jason Staples, before 1840, in Baldwin County[48], died unknown.

1860

Monroe County, Alabama[49]

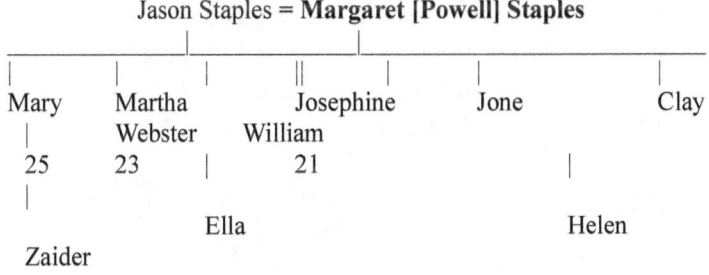

```
            Jason Staples = Margaret [Powell] Staples
       _____|_____|_____
       |       |         ||       |         |             |
      Mary   Martha   Josephine   Jone                   Clay
       |     Webster   William                            |
       25      23         21                              |
       |                  |                               |
                         Ella                           Helen
     Zaider
```

Heiress Mary Delphine Saunders

Margaret Tate's daughter by William Theophilus Powell, Mary Delphine Powell, born 1809, in South Carolina [Alabama], married David Moniac, in Baldwin County, in 1828.⁵⁰ [Moniac Saunders] Starke, lived in Monroe County, near her mother, at Montpelier, prior to moving to Baldwin County. Mary D. Starke was enumerated as "Indian," in the 1860 Census for Alabama.⁵¹ Mary Starke received her widow's pension for famous first husband, David Moniac.⁵² David Moniac, David Tate's nephew, was the first "Indian" to attend and graduate from West Point Military Academy.

Tate wrote his nephew, in 1822, alerting him to the dissipation of personal and real property that his father, Sam Moniac was experiencing at home. Land grabbers had reduced his father to poverty, and Tate was concerned that David Moniac would be totally bankrupt upon his return. Moniac left West Point early, after graduating at the bottom of his class. He re-enlisted in time to fight the Florida Wars against the Seminoles, where he died in action, in 1836.

1860
*Baldwin County, Alabama*⁵³

Turner Starke = Mary Delphine [Powell] Starke
―――――――――――――――――――
| | |
David A. Moniac   A. C. Moniac

1870
Township 4, Baker [Baldwin]County, Alabama

```
                    Mary Stark[e] = Turner Stark[e]⁵⁴
_____60_____|_____75_____
       |              |             |              |
Alex   Ann C Moniac   Frank Stark   Frozine McGee  Caroline
                                                   McGee
Jack                                                        Stark
                                                   Black
       Domestic
```

William Theophilus Powell
Heir of Reuben Dyer and
William T. Powell of McIntosh's Bluff

Margaret Tate's only son, William Thelps [Theophilus] Powell [III], a Creek-Choctaw metis, b. 1812, married Martha A. Bryant,[55] another Choctaw-metis, died August 31, 1852, in Alabama, was the father of Robert, Fredonia, and Marsalina [Marchanna],[56] all lost to the record. William's father was William Theophilus Powell, [II], died circa 1816, during the First Seminole War. William Powell [II], was the cousin of another William "Billy" Powell Red Stick leader, Osceola. The first recorded William Powell [I], died, the owner of a 1797 Spanish Land Grant, along the Tombigbee River, affirmed in 1804.[57] William T. Powell [II] was not his father's firstborn son, thus, his wealth came primarily from his wife's property.[58] Indeed, he was not included in the Will of William Powell, born 1712, at McIntosh Bluff, died 1796, in Washington County, Mississippi Territory. Possibly, he was unrelated to Powell's widow, Elizabeth Nash; but, rather was the son of another wife. That would explain his disinheritance. William Theophilus Powell [II] returned Dyer's property to her in his Will of 1816. Margaret Dyer Powell, lost nothing at the death of her mother, Mary [Cussins] Dyer and husband, except a fifty percent share to her dependent sister, Martha "Polly" Dyer.

Also, the minor Powell differentiated himself from another Wm. Powell, of Baldwin County. He styled himself, W.T. The other Powell married Mary Ship, October 11, 1849. A.B. Couch officiated.[59]

William Theophilus Powell [III], had eight slaves in 1850.[60] [61] His children received the following slaves from his mother upon her death in 1851:[62]

*children of
beloved son, William T.
Powell*

William	*one negro man*
Aaron	*one negro man*
Cuff	*one negro man*
Stephen	*one negro boy*
{Elouisa	*one negro woman*
Siky	*and her four children*
Daphney	
Chloe	
Tab} family unit	
Poss	*one negro woman*

In 1852, William T. Powell, followed his mother in death.[63] His demise caused quite a stir, since he died intestate (without a will). A lawsuit ensued, reportedly to recover any mismanaged capital or chattel property not only from Powell's estate, but also from that of his mother, Margaret Tate. Powell's estate was significant because of the presence of former Tate slaves. After all, we want to know what became of Tate's slaves, four of whom were direct antecedents.

Powell's Probate file was mislabeled as 1832. His file had been conflated with that of his father, T. Powell who died in 1816 or 1817.

Exactly one month after the demise of Powell, on September 28, 1852, James Dreisbach made his preemptive strike. He was the first to address the Court, in his bid to be named Administrator; a blatant attempt to beat Martha Crow, Powell's newly-married widow to the punch. His return address was Mount Pleasant, P.O. Monroe County.

September 28, 1852[64]

Hon Judge Byrne

Dear Sir,

I wish to take out letters of administration on the Estate of W.T. Powell, and the Estate of W.T. Powell's children. It is highly important that someone should take charge of the effects as soon as possible as the interests of the claimants demand it at as early period as possible [sic], I learned yesterday that the widow had no intention of Administering. You will please let me know by return mail how many days notice will be given the widow before you can grant letters to me, provided she does not come forward and take out letters herself. In the event that letters are granted to me, you will please give me instructions about my bond, etc. By giving the above your early attention you are much obliged.

Your obedient servant [sic]
<u>J. D. Dreisbach</u>

Direct your letters to Mount Pleasant, P.O. Monroe Co.

The Dreisbachs apparently resided at Montpelier, otherwise known as Mount Pleasant. Margaret Tate died in 1851, and Josephine was naturally, her immediate heir. After eight years of marriage, Dreisbach was not hesitant to assert his rights over his wife's inheritance. To the Dreisbachs' consternation, however, on October 22, 1852, Dr. William Wilkins was appointed Administrator of Powell's Estate. Wilkins' appointment was the instant wish of Powell's widow, Martha *[Bryant Powell]* Crow, at a hearing held October 16, 1852. Though illiterate, she would not be outdone.

State of Alabama)
Baldwin County) *To the Honorable Patrick Byrne, Judge*[65]

if the Probate Court of said County, in the State of aforesaid,
   Your Petitioner,
      Martha Powell would respectfully shew [sic]
unto your Honor that Mr. Wm. T. Powell departed this life at his residence in said County on the 31st day of August last intestate, that he left an estate both real and personal and that there has been no administration on the same, that she is the widow of said Wm. T. Powell, for such widow is entitled to the administration of said estate, and therefore claimed the right of nominating as administrator William Wilkins, whose experience in such matters qualifies him to discharge the duties of said office in accordance with Law and that she verily believes that it is for the best interest of the Estate and the heirs at Law that said William Wilkins be appointed as administrator of said Estate.
   And as is duly bound Will ever pray, etc.

          her
Martha X mark Powell

Blakely, Ala.
October 16, 1852
Witness:
Elizabeth C. Benjee [sic]

Wilkins, brother of Judge Charles W. Wilkins, thought it necessary to retain his own attorney, O. C. Hall. A number of sundry debtors surfaced for payment. Charles Weatherford, manager, Josephine's uncle, was one of many paid by Powell's Estate. Weatherford was paid $80.00 as acting overseer on the plantation, January 15, 1853. George Daffin, another overseer, received $13.00, February 19, 1853, for "one month's service." Others were: C. Daniels, Justice of the Peace, Edward Steadham, Jason Staples, Holden Oguirne, John Blake, Richard Moore, Benjamin N. Davis, Thomas Byrne, Elisha Tarvin, and Young C. Hall.

The Estate was appraised at $11,000 for the value of the slaves alone. The Dreisbachs and Martha Bryant Powell Crow divided 18 slaves, and received $429.34 each. William Neal *[sic]*, was sold on January 14, 1856, for $800.00, to Francis Earl[e]. Lucy and child Cuff, were sold to James Vaughn, on the same date, for $1,015.00,[66] to satisfy a $1400.00 debt.

In Petition 20185414, the Dreisbachs initially named 39 slaves. They subsequently amended their Petition to include only 20 slaves. There was little overlap in the named slaves. That is only three slaves were named in the Dreisbachs' Petition, that were also persons enumerated in either Margaret Tate's Will or William T. Powell's Estate. Eleven female juvenile slaves were missing from the slave inventory at the final disposition of Powell's Estate. Those young women were likely David Tate's daughters, and not slaves. There was no accounting for the original 100 slaves, enumerated in the Slave Inventory of 1829. The following table shows the distribution of slaves at the conclusion of the lawsuit, and division of property. The first group went to the Dreisbachs.

Table 1.   Enumerated in Tate's Will?

	Name	Age in 1856	Enumerated in Tate's Will?[67]
1)	Hannah	55	NO
2)	Sam	35	YES
3)	Jim	20	NO
4)	Elouisa	29	YES
5)	child Jack		NO
6)	Daphne	6	YES
7)	Tab	3	YES
8)	Yellow Cuff	35	YES
9)	Young Poss	3 mos	NO

And the following to Martha Powell Crow:[68]

	Name	Age in 1856	Enumerated in Tate's Will?
1)	Abby and	25	NO
2)	child		NO
3)	Boy Primus	10	NO
4)	Girl Hannah	9	NO
5)	Sarah	18 mos	NO
6)	Chloe	7	YES
7)	Man Stephen	16	YES
8)	Old Poss	45	YES
9)	Aaron	50	YES

Shipping Cotton by Torchlight on the Alabama River. Courtesy the New York Public Library, Digital Collections.

Conclusion

A mixed-blood girl came of age along the Gulf borderlands, during the most turbulent period of American history. Margaret Dyer was born a Choctaw metis, and breathed life under Spanish dominion. She witnessed unbridled American intrigues to replace rival powers, both foreign and domestic. Born in a time of "manifest destiny," she witnessed the usurpation of indigenous peoples, her own, the Five Civilized Tribes. In her time, patriotism was served hot with a hymn. She encountered former Vice President, Aaron Burr, before his arrest for treason; and future President Andrew Jackson, as he murdered countless Creek women and children, with gloved hands. Endowed with slaves and wealth, she wined and dined Spanish governors, Dons, American and British interlopers. Margaret Dyer-Powell, like most women, sat behind heavy drapes, while men smoked and designed machinations before flickering candles, sipping brandy.

Appropriately, she feigned illiteracy, to disarm discerning chauvinists. When pressed, Tate rose to the task of guardianship for her young daughter. She was the mistress of a cotton plantation. Her brother-in-law, Charles Weatherford served as overseer, until her son reached maturity. The widow and relic of two powerful Indian men, she suffered the brutal deaths of her mother and sister, at Fort Mims. Her world encompassed the perplexities of the Native American mixed-blood at the height of American expansionism. How did she feel about the invading country? What were her true allegiances? Had her family's losses engendered a vendetta mindset? Was she aware of her place in the scheme of things? Or, was she a totally acculturated sellout?

Selected Bibliography

AccessGenealogy.com. Web. 27 March 2015.
http://www.accessgenealogy.com/native/final-rolls.htm - Last updated on Oct 4th, 2013

MariLee Beatty Hageness, *Alabama Genealogical Sources, Abstracts of Will Book A, 1809-1881, Mississippi Territory & Baldwin County, Alabama. Volume AL4-2*, Privately published 1995.

Kathryn E. Holland Braund, "Guardians of Tradition and Handmaidens to Change: Women's Roles in Creek Economic and Social Life During the Eighteenth Century," *American Indian Quarterly Summer90, Vol. 14 Issue 3,* p239-258. 20p.

Willis Brewer, *Alabama, her history, resources, war record, and public men : from 1540 to 1872,* Montgomery, Ala: Barrett & Brown, 1872. 29-30.

James F. Brooks, Ed., *Confounding the Color Line: the Indian-Black experience in North America*, July 1, 2002.

William E. Coffer (Koi Hosh), *Phoenix : The Decline and Rebirth of the Indian People,* Van Nostrand Reinhold Co., 1979, Appendix, page 251-252.

Robert S. Cotterill, "A Chapter of Panton, Leslie and Company," *The Journal of Southern History, Vol. 10. No.3 (Aug., 1944...), * at http://jstor.org/discover/10.2307/2197938?sid=21105779143...

Karl Davis, "Remember Fort Mims:" Reinterpreting the Origins of the Creek War," *Journal of the Early Republic,* Vol. 22, No. 4 (Winter, 2002).

Gilbert C. Din, *War on the Gulf Coast: The Spanish Fight against William Augustus Bowles,"* University Press of Florida, c. 2012. Pp. [xiv]. 319.

Gregory E. Dowd, *A Spirited Resistance: The North American Indian Struggle for Unity, 1745-1815* (The Johns Hopkins University Studies in Historical and Political Science), 1991.

John T. Ellisor, *The Second Creek War: interethnic conflict and collusion on a collapsing frontier,* (Indians of the Southeast), Nov 1, 2010.

Robbie Etheridge, *Creek Country: The Creek Indians and Their World*, The University of North Carolina Press, 2003.

Jack D. Forbes, *Africans and Native Americans: the language of race and the evolution of Red-Black peoples,* March 1, 1993.

Carolyn Thomas Foreman, "The Brave Major Moniac and the Creek Volunteers," *Chonicles of Oklahoma,* http://digital.library.okstate.edu/Chronicles/v023/v023p096.pdf, (accessed March 2015).

Carolyn Thomas Foreman, "The White Lieutenant and Some of His Contemporaries," *Chonicles of Oklahoma,*digital.library.okstate.edu/Chronicles/v038/v038p425.pdf (accessed April 2015).

Andrew K. Frank, *Creeks and Southerners: Biculturalism on the*

Early American Frontier
Lincoln, Neb., 2005.

Michael D. Green, *The Politics of Indian Removal : Creek Government and Society in Crisis,"* University of Nebraska Press, 1985.

Cindy Griffin and Sherry Hicks, *1789 Catholic Baptisms for Tombigbee, Tensaw and Alabama River Settlements*, [Guillermo, Isabel and Sara Dyer, children of Ruben Dyer and Maria Cupins [Cusins], from Vida's Legacy, http://vidas.rootsweb.ancestry.com/catbap1789.html (accessed March 2014).

Peter J. Hamilton, *Colonial Mobile : an historical study, largely from original sources, of the Alabama-Tombigbee Basin and the old South West from the discovery of the Spiritu Santo in 1519 until the demolition of Fort Charlotte in 1821,* Boston: Houghton Mifflin, 1910.

Benjamin Hawkins, *A Sketch of the Creek Country in the Years 1798 and 1799*, in Collections of the Georgia Historical Society, vol. 3, pt. 1 (Savannah, Ga., 1971), 37–39.

Lawrence M. Hauptman and Heriberto Dixon, "Cadet David Moniac: A Creek Indian's Schooling at West Point, 1817-1822, *Proceedings of the American Philosophical Society, Vol. 152, No. 3*, September 2008.pg. 330; Gilbert Russell to Wm. H. Crawford, 1 March 1816.

Robert V. Haynes, *The Mississippi Territory and the Southwest Frontier, 1795-1817,* University Press of Kentucky, September 2010, Pages: 432

Florette Henri, *The Southern Indians and Benjamin Hawkins, 1796– 1816*, May, 1986, 284–85.

Horton, James Oliver and Lois E. Horton, *Slavery and the Making of America* (New York: Oxford university Press, 2005), pp 81–83

Angela Pulley Hudson, *Creek Paths and Federal Roads Indians, Settlers, and Slaves and the Making of the American South*, University of North Carolina Press, June 2010, Pages: 272.

James Innerarity, "General Wilkinson's Occupation of Mobile, April, 1813: A letter of James Innerarity to John Forbes," *The Florida Historical Society Quarterly*, Vol. 11, No. 2 (Oct., 1932), pp. 88-90.

Charles J. Kappler, *Indian Affairs, Laws and Treaties, Volume 2: Treaties* (Senate, 57th Congress, Doc. 452) 1903, The Treaty of Fort Jackson.

Almon Wheeler Lauber, *Indian slavery in colonial times within the present limits of the United States*, May 20, 2009.

Daniel F. Littlefield, *Africans and Creeks: from the colonial period to the Civil War*, Greenwood Press, 1979, 286 pages.

Katja May, *African Americans and Native Americans in the Creek and Cherokee Nations, 1830s, to 1920s : collision and collusion*, (Studies in African American History and Culture), January, 1996.

Edwin C. McReynolds, *The Seminoles*, University of Oklahoma Press, 1957, page 54.

Kay Nuzum, *A History of Baldwin County,"* Page & Palette, Inc., 1971.

Frank L. Owsley Jr, *Struggle for the Gulf Borderlands: The Creek War and the Battle of New Orleans, 1812-1815,* September 8, 2000, 38–39.

Paredes, J. Anthony and Knight, *Red Eagle's Children, Weatherford vs. Weatherford, et al.* (Contemporary American Indians) Hardcover – October 16, 2012.

Pickett, A. J. *Interesting Notes upon the History of Alabama.*

Daniel K. Richter, *Facing East from Indian Country : A Native History of Early America,* Harvard University Press, 2001.

James Roberts, b. 1753, *The Narrative of James Roberts, a Soldier Under Gen. Washington in the Revolutionary War, and Under Gen. Jackson at the Battle of New Orleans, in the War of 1812: "a Battle Which Cost Me a Limb, Some Blood, and Almost My Life,"* Chicago: Author, 1858.

Adam Rothman, *Slave country: American expansion and the origins of the Deep South,* May 30, 2007.

Claudio Saunt, "Taking Account of Property: Stratification among the Creek Indians in the Early Nineteenth Century," *The William and Mary quarterly, Third Series, Vol. 57, (Oct., 2000), pp. 733-760*

Claudio Saunt, *A New Order of Things: Property, Power, and the Transformation of the Creek Indians, 1733-1816 (Studies in North American Indian History), August 28, 1999, 271–72;*

Royce Gordon Shingleton, "David Brydie Mitchell and the African Importation Case of 1820, " *The Journal of Negro History, Vol. 58, No. 3 (Jul., 1973),* pp. 327-340.

Deanna M. Slappey, "Mary Cussins, Mother of Tensaw Settlement Survivors Margaret (Dryer) Powell and Martha (Dyer) Weatherford," *National Genealogical Society Quarterly 99 (March 2011)*; 43-58.

Elizabeth Shown Mills, "Documenting a Slave's Birth, Parentage, and Origins (Marie Thérèse Coincoin, 1742–1816): A Test of Oral History." *National Genealogical Society Quarterly* 96 (December 2008): 245–66. Digital image. Elizabeth Shown Mills, *Historic*

Pathways. http://www.HistoricPathways.com : December 2014;

J. Leitch Wright Jr., "Creek-American Treaty of 1790: Alexander McGillivray and The Diplomacy of The Old Southwest," *The Georgia Historical Quarterly, Vol. 51, No. 4 (December, 1967), pp. 379-400*

J. Leitch Wright Jr., *Creeks and Seminoles: The Destruction and Regeneration of the Muscogulge People, (Indians of the Southeast),* Lincoln, Neb., 1986, 166–82;

Phillip W. McMullin, editor, "Grassroots of America," A Computerized Index to the American State Papers: Land Grants and Claims (1789 - 1837) With Other Aids to Research, (Government document serial set numbers 28 through 36), Second Reprinting 1994 with special permission by: Southern Historical Press, Inc., Arkansas Research, Conway, AR.

Elizabeth Shown Mills and Rachal Mills Lennon. "Mother, Thy Name Is *Mystery!* Finding the Slave Who Bore Philomene Daurat." *Reconstructing Female Lives: A Special Issue of the National Genealogical Society Quarterly 88* (September 2000): 201–24.

Elizabeth Shown Mills, "Roundabout Research: Pursuing Collateral Lines to Prove Parentage of a Direct Ancestor—Samuel Hanson of Frontier Georgia." *National Genealogical Society Quarterly* 91 (March 2003): 19–30;

Elizabeth Shown Mills, "Spanish Records: Locating Anglo and Latin Ancestry in the Colonial Southeast." *National Genealogical Society Quarterly* 73 (December 1985): 243–61;

Elizabeth Shown Mills, *QuickSheet: The Historical Biographer's Guide to Cluster Research (the FAN Principle)* (Baltimore: GPC, 2012).

Christina Snyder, "Conquered Enemies, Adopted Kin, and Owned People: The Creek Indians and Their Captives," *Journal of Southern History. May2007, Vol. 73 Issue 2, p255-288.*

Stiggins, George *Creek Indian History: A Historical Narrative of the Genealogy, Traditions, and Downfall of the Ispocoga Or Creek Indian Tribe of Indians* Birmingham Public Library Press, 1989,

John Sugden, *Tecumseh: A Life,* Macmillan, Apr 15, 1999, 492 pages. Page 248-250.

Lynn Hastie Thompson, "William Weatherford, His Country and His People," Lavender Publishing Company; 2nd edition (1991).

United States. Congress. *Letter from the Secretary of the Treasury Relative to ... an Act for the Relief of Samuel Menac, Passed 27th of April 1816; Also, of an Act for the Relief of Certain Creek Indians, Passed 3d March, 1817,* 20th Cong, 1st session, House Document 200. Washington: Gales & Seaton, 1828.

"Letter from the Secretary of the Treasury, transmitting The Information Required by a Resolution of the House of Representatives, of the 3d Instant, Relative to the Execution of *An Act for the Relief of Samuel Menac, Passed 27th of April, 1816:* Also of an *Act for the Relief of Certain Creek Indians, Passed 3d March, 1817, &c. &c. March 15, 1828. . . . Indemnity for Damages by Creek Indians*, 20th Congress, 1st Session. [Doc. No. 200.] Ho. of Reps. Treas'y Dept. 1828. Pages 1-13. At: www.findingsouthernancestors.com/download/act.pdf

United States Bureau of Indian Affairs, *Recommendation and summary of evidence for proposed finding for Federal acknowledgment of the Poarch Band of Creeks of Alabama pursuant to 25 CFR 83.* United States Department of the Interior, Office of Federal Acknowledgement ...... *and recommended that the children of Semoice be given patents, Dec. 29, 1983,* www.bia.gov/cs/.../idc-001321.pdf (accessed January 2014).

T.S. Woodward, *Woodward's reminiscences of the Creek or Muscogee Indians contained in letters to friends in Georgia and Alabama by Thomas S. Woodward, of Louisiana (formerly of Alabama) ; with an appendix containing interesting matter relating to the general subject.* Published 1859 by Barrett & Wimbish

Amos J. Wright, Jr., *The McGillivray and McIntosh Traders: On the Old Southwest Frontier 1716-1815 (Google eBook),* NewSouth Books, Feb 1, 2007, 332 pages.

J. Leitch Wright, Jr., *Creeks and Seminoles, The Destruction and Regeneration of the Muscogulge People,* University of Nebraska Press, 1990.

SOURCES

1. "Known and Probable Mixed-bloods," Database of Choctaw Mixed Blood Names, Choctaw Mixed Bloods; Wells, Dr. Samuel James. *Choctaw Mixed Bloods and the Advent of Removal.* University of Southern Mississippi. 1987. © Dr. Samuel James Wells, 1987. Used by permission. AccessGenealogy.com. Web. 19 June 2016. https://www.accessgenealogy.com/native/database-of-choctaw-mixed-blood-names.htm
2. "Sept 27, 1830 Treaty of Dancing Rabbit Creek, Bureau of Indian Affairs NARA," *Historical Records: Bureau of Indian Affairs Commissioners of Indian Affairs NARA National Archives Records Adm. Washington DC,* http://sept271830treatyofdancingrabbitcreek.blogspot.com/
3. Carolyn E. Hood-Kourdache, *David Tate: Origins*, 2016.
4. Lackey, Richard S., "Frontier Claims in the Lower South," Polyanthos, 1977, page 49. "Mary Dryer [Dyer].
5. American State Papers, Public Lands, Volume 4, page 502-503: William Collins.
6. "Alabama Estate Files, 1830-1976," database with images, *FamilySearch* (https://familysearch.org/ark:/61903/1:1:VNTV-ZWN : 12 December 2014), Josephine Tate, 1832; citing Baldwin County courthouse, Alabama; FHL microfilm 2,363,134.
7. Cummins, Light Townsend *The Other War of 1812: The Patriot War and the American Invasion of Spanish East Florida (review), From: The Americas Volume 61, Number 4, April 2005 pp. 721-722 | 10.1353/tam.2005.0070* http://muse.jhu.edu/article/182050
8. "United States Census, 1850," database with images, *FamilySearch* (https://familysearch.org/ark:/61903/1:1:MHP5-93L : 9 November 2014), Fredonia Powell in household of W T Powell, Baldwin county, Baldwin, Alabama, United States; citing family 42, NARA microfilm publication M432 (Washington, D.C.: National Archives and Records Administration, n.d.).
9. Louis Marchand, Baldwin County Department of Archives and History, Miscellaneous Court Records 1801-1825, Box #1: Contains 34 folders, Lawsuit, June 3, 1823, Louis Marchand vs. Abigail Spalding and Edward Furman [for rent], 1821, Special Edition Folder 27. Apparently, Louis Marchand had legal issue that still resided in Baldwin County, as late as 1823. One may

SOURCES

deduce that Marchand was not married to the original Sehoy. or had multiple wives.
10 Wright, *The McGillivray and McIntosh Traders*, pg. 194.
11 Linda Langley, *The Tribal Identity of Alexander McGillivray:*
12 "Narrative of John Davis," *Southwestern Monthly, Vol. 1, pp. 213-214*. It is uncertain which, and how many, of the Castlemans were present. Mr. Davis, speaking many years afterwards, mentions John, Sr., Joseph, and David. General Robertson, in reporting the ed. (*American State Papers, Indian Affairs, Vol. 1, p. 466.*) David Wilson, in a contemporary letter, says Jacob was killed and Joseph wounded. (American Historical Magazine, Vol. 2, p. 94.) Mrs. Sallie Smith, in a letter to her husband, General Daniel Smith, says two of the young Castlemans were killed and old Honnis wounded. (American Historical Magazine. Vol. 5. p. 293.) ^American State Papers, Indian Affairs, Vol. 1, p. 472; Haywood's Civil and Political History of Tennessee, p. 387. "James Robertson, American State Papers, Indian Affairs, Vol. 1, p. 467; Haywood's Civil and Political History of Tennessee, p. 384. Important to this work is who the Creeks were that were ambushed. Apparently, at least one of those killed was a son of the White Lieutenant.
13 Christina Snyder, "Conquered Enemies, Adopted Kin, and Owned People: The Creek Indians and Their Captives, " *Journal of Southern History. May2007, Vol. 73 Issue 2, p255-288.*
14 George Stiggins was the son of Joseph Stiggins, and his Indian wife Haw. Joseph Stiggins purchased his land from Reuben Dyer, Margaret's father. Stiggins remained her lifelong friend, until his death in 1845, having written his "History of the Creeks . . . "
15 The Library of Congress, "A Century of Lawmaking for a New Nation: U.S. Congressional Documents and Debates, 1774 - 1885," *Journal of the House of Representatives of the United States, Volume 11, Page 56 of 606.* at: http://memory.loc.gov/cgi-bin/ampage?collid... Accessed: October 2015.
16 Estate Records of Theophilus Powell, Monroe County, Alabama, Orphans Court Record of Orders Book No. 1 1816 - 1821, FHL #1548209.
17 1810 Census Baldwin County, Alabama, Baldwin County

SOURCES

Genealogical Society, for Mary Dyer, dead URL. Now at Ancestry.com. *Alabama, Compiled Census and Census Substitutes Index, 1810-1890* [database on-line]. Provo, UT, USA: Ancestry.com Operations Inc, 1999.

18 Bureau of Land Managment, General Land Office Records, Mary Dyer, Patent Image, at http://www.glorecords.blm.gov/details/patent/default.aspx?accession=AL5210__.033&docClass=STA&sid=3aydcdfe.fvj, (accessed December 2014).

19 Adam Rothman, *Slave Country, : American Expansion and the Origins of the Deep South,* Harvard University Press, 2005. page 137.

20 Theophilus Powell, Last Will and Testament, May 17, 1816, Monroe County, Alabama, Orphans Court Record of Orders Book No. 1. 1816-1821. FHL# 1548209.

21 Paredes, J. Anthony and Knight, *Red Eagle's Children, Weatherford vs. Weatherford, et al.* (Contemporary American Indians) Hardcover – October 16, 2012.

22 Peter J Hamilton, C*olonial Mobile : an historical study, largely from original sources, of the Alabama-Tombigbee Basin and the old South West from the discovery of the Spiritu Santo in 1519 until the demolition of Fort Charlotte in 1821, Boston: Houghton Mifflin, 1910,* In The Creole Country, page 519. Pierre Juzan was an Indian interpreter. page 362.

23 William E. Coffer (Koi Hosh), *Phoenix : The Decline and Rebirth of the Indian People,* Van Nostrand Reinhold Co., 1979, Appendix, page 251-252. Pierre Juzan signed the Treaty of Dancing Rabbit Creek, 1830; and received a section of land for his service.

24 "Alabama, County Marriages, 1809-1950," David Tate and Penny Coleman, 25 Jun 1814; citing Mobile, Alabama, United States, county courthouses, Alabama; FHL microfilm 2,218,267 (accessed 12 December 2014),

25 Hood-Kourdache, *David Tate : Origins. 2016*

26 Oral history as told by Rev. John Seth Bailey of Bailey's Temple, Detroit Michigan, in 1979.

27 "Alabama Estate Files, 1830-1976," database with images, *FamilySearch* (https://familysearch.org/ark:/61903/1:1:VNTV-

SOURCES

ZWN : 12 December 2014), Josephine Tate, 1832; citing Baldwin County courthouse, Alabama; FHL microfilm 2,363,134. Image 72 of 95.
28 American State Papers: Documents, Legislative and Executive, of ..., Volume 33, By United States. CongressGales and Seaton, 1860 - Archives, https://books.google.com/books.
29 Margaret Tate, Last Will and Testament, Will Book "A," Baldwin County, Alabama pg. 116-119, 27th March, 1851.
30 Ibid.
31 Margaret Tate, Last Will and Testament.
32 Bureau of Land Management, BLM.gov, http://www.glorecords.blm.gov/results/default.aspx?searchCriteria=type=patent|st=AL|cty=003|ln=tate|sp=true|sw=true|sadv=false
33 Ibid.
34 University of Alabama : http://alabamamaps.ua.edu/contemporarymaps/alabama/basemaps/index.html (accessed 04 Nov 2013).
35 Bureau of Land Management, BLM.gov.
36 Alabama, Estate Files, 1830-1976, index and images, *FamilySearch* (https://familysearch.org/pal:/MM9.1.1/VNTV-Z4R (accessed 26 January 2015), Josephine B Dreisbach, 1908; citing Baldwin County, county courthouses, Alabama; FHL microfilm 2,363,136.
37 "United States Census, 1880," Josephine Dreisbach in household of Jas Dreisbach, Montgomery Hill, Baldwin, Alabama, United States; citing enumeration district 1, sheet 147A, NARA microfilm publication T9 (Washington D.C.: National Archives and Records Administration, n.d.), roll 0001; FHL microfilm 1,254,001.
38 "United States Census, 1880," Thaddeus Tate, Montgomery Hill, Baldwin, Alabama, United States; citing enumeration district 1, sheet 147A, NARA microfilm publication T9 (Washington D.C.: National Archives and Records Administration, n.d.), roll 0001; FHL microfilm 1,254,001.
39 "United States Census, 1860," index, *FamilySearch* (https://familysearch.org/pal:/MM9.1.1/MHD4-GKK (accessed 26 January 2015), Josephene B Dreesbach in household of J D

SOURCES

Dreesbach, , Baldwin, Alabama, United States; from "1860 U.S. Federal Census - Population," *Fold3.com*; citing p. 83, household ID 542, NARA microfilm publication M653, National Archives and Records Administration, Washington, D.C.; FHL microfilm 803,001.

40 "United States Census, 1870," index and images, *FamilySearch* (https://familysearch.org/pal:/MM9.1.1/MHKH-JM2 (accessed 26 January 2015), Josephine Dresback in household of James D Dresback, Alabama, United States; citing p. 2, family 12, NARA microfilm publication M593 (Washington D.C.: National Archives and Records Administration, n.d.); FHL microfilm 545,500.

41 "Alabama, Deaths, 1908-1974," Mary Staples, 18 Jul 1922; citing reference cn 12418, Department of Health, Montgomery; FHL microfilm 1,908,240.

42 "United States Census, 1860," (accessed 28 January 2015), Josephine Staples in household of Jason Staples, , Monroe, Alabama, United States; from "1860 U.S. Federal Census - Population," *Fold3.com*; citing p. 106, household ID 725, NARA microfilm publication M653, National Archives and Records Administration, Washington, D.C.; FHL microfilm 803,018.

43 "United States Census, 1870, Mary J Staples in household of Margart Staples, Alabama, United States; citing p. 1, family 5, NARA microfilm publication M593 (Washington D.C.: National Archives and Records Administration, n.d.); FHL microfilm 545,531.

44 Ibid.

45 "United States Census, 1880," Mary Staples in household of Margaret Staples, Montgomery Hill, Baldwin, Alabama, United States; citing enumeration district 1, sheet 147B, NARA microfilm publication T9 (Washington D.C.: National Archives and Records Administration, n.d.), roll 0001; FHL microfilm 1,254,001.

46 "United States Census, 1860," index, *FamilySearch* (https://familysearch.org/pal:/MM9.1.1/MHDX-ZXM (accessed 28 January 2015), Josephine Staples in household of Jason Staples, , Monroe, Alabama, United States; from "1860 U.S. Federal Census - Population," *Fold3.com*; citing p. 106, household ID 725, NARA microfilm publication M653, National Archives and Records Administration, Washington, D.C.; FHL microfilm 803,018.

47 "United States Census, 1880," Margaret Staples, Montgomery Hill, Baldwin, Alabama, United States; citing enumeration district 1, sheet 147B, NARA microfilm publication T9 (Washington D.C.: National Archives and Records Administration, n.d.), roll 0001; FHL microfilm 1,254,001.

48 "United States Census, 1840," Jason Staples, Not Stated, Baldwin, Alabama; citing p. 91, NARA microfilm publication M704, (Washington D.C.: National Archives and Records Administration, n.d.), roll 1; FHL microfilm 2,332.

SOURCES

49 "United States Census, 1860," Josephine Staples in household of Jason Staples, , Monroe, Alabama, United States; from "1860 U.S. Federal Census - Population," *Fold3.com*; citing p. 106, household ID 725, NARA microfilm publication M653, National Archives and Records Administration, Washington, D.C.; FHL microfilm 803,018.

50 "Alabama, County Marriages, 1809-1950," (accessed 4 February 2015), David Manias [Moniac] and Mary Delphine Powell, 25 Sep 1828; citing Baldwin, Alabama, United States, county courthouses, Alabama; FHL microfilm 1,839,621.

51 "United States Census, 1860," (accessed 13 December 2014, Mary D Starke in household of Turner Starke, , Baldwin, Alabama, United States; from "1860 U.S. Federal Census - Population," *Fold3.com*; p. 29, household ID 193, NARA microfilm publication M653; NARA microfilm publication M653. National Archives and Records Administration, Washington, D.C.; FHL microfilm 803,001. ["other"]

52 "United States Old War Pension Index, 1815-1926," index and images, *FamilySearch* (https://familysearch.org/pal:/MM9.1.1/KZPT-1M5 (accessed 13 December 2014), Mary D Starke in entry for David Moniar, 1851; citing Pension, Alabama, NARA microfilm publication T316, National Archives and Records Administration, Washington D.C.; FHL microfilm 821,607.

53 "United States Census, 1860," Mary D Starke in household of Turner Starke, , Baldwin, Alabama, United States; from "1860 U.S. Federal Census - Population," *Fold3.com*; citing p. 29, household ID 193, NARA microfilm publication M653, National Archives and Records Administration, Washington, D.C.; FHL microfilm 803,001.

54 "United States Census, 1870," database with images, *FamilySearch* (https://familysearch.org/ark:/61903/1:1:MHK4-5RV : accessed 13 June 2016), Turner Stark in household of Alex Moniac, Alabama, United States; citing p. 3, family 17, NARA microfilm publication M593 (Washington D.C.: National Archives and Records Administration, n.d.); FHL microfilm 545,500.

55 Martha Bryant, Last Will and Testament, Baldwin County, Alabama. Found at: accessGenealogy.com. http://files.usgwarchives.net/al/baldwin/wills/mbryant.txt, for

SOURCES

Baldwin County Wills. accessed: November 2014. "*devised to my daughters Louisa Daniels formerly Bryant and* **Martha Powell** *formerly Bryant...* " 1848.

56 "United States Census, 1850," Robert Powell in household of W T Powell, Baldwin county, Baldwin, Alabama, United States; citing dwelling 42, family 42, NARA microfilm publication M432, roll 1.

57 "Spanish and British Land Grants in Mississippi Territory. 1750 - 1784" [database on-line], Provo, UT USA. *The Generations Ntwork, Inc.,* 2006. Ancestry.com.
Original data: Clifford Neal Smith, *Spanish and British Land Grants in Mississippi Territory, 1750-1784*. Baltimore, MC, USA: Genealogical Publishing Co., 2004.

58 [William] Theophilus Powell, Last Will and Testament, [William Powell of McIntosh Bluff] January 23, 1796

59 "Alabama, County Marriages, 1809-1950", database with images, *FamilySearch* (https://familysearch.org/ark:/61903/1:1:XTWT-K49 : 16 July 2015), William Powell and Mary Ship, 1849.

60 "United States Census (Slave Schedule), 1850 ," W T Powell, 1850.

61 "Alabama, Estate Files, 1830-1976," William T Powell, 1832. The file should be corrected to read "1852."

62 Margaret Tate's Last Will and Testament.

63 Recorded in Book "H," the Orphans Court, Baldwin County, found at: "Alabama, Estate Files, 1830-1976," index and images, *FamilySearch* (https://familysearch.org/pal:/MM9.1.1/VNTV-C4M : accessed 30 Oct 2013), William T Powell, 1832 [1852].

64 William T. Powell, Alabama Estate Files 1830-1976, Baldwin County, Alabama, image 70 of 114, accessed: November 2014.

65 Ibid. 66 of 114.

66 William T. Powell Estate, recorded in Book "A," page 53-54, the Orphans Court, Baldwin County, January 14, 1856.

67 Martha Tate Last Will & Testament.

68 "Alabama, Estate Files, 1830-1976," William T Powell, 1832

SOURCES

Alphabetical Index

1810 Mississippi Territorial Census....................................25
Aaron Burr..38
acculturated...14
acres...17
Act of Congress..34, 40
Adam Hollinger..43
adjoining..21
administration...37
AfroCreek metis...30
Alexander...29
American Patriots..23
Amey...40
an Act making provision..40
Anderson..35
Annexation...33
appropriated..21
Arkansas...17
arrest..38
Arthur Sizemore...38
August 30, 1813..20
Bayou Boeuf...21
Bella..36
Ben..35
Ben Durant...29
Benjamin Hawkins...18
bequeathed...22
black slavery..21
blacksmith..36
Bonaparte...40
border...18
British trader...13
Bryant...26
Burnt Corn Creek...33
capture...18
cede..20

SOURCES

cessation..39
Charles Weatherford...29
Chief Malcolm McPherson..29
chieftain...21
Choctaw bride..13
Choctaw metis..14, 40
Choctaw mixed-blood...13
Choctaw Nation...13
Choctaw Treaties..17
Choctaw-metis...13
christening...20
citizens..17
citizenship...17
claimant..21
Col. David Tait...29
Commissioner Plenipoteniary....................................18
concubine..20, 41
contempt...44
Cornelius Rains...38
countrymen...41
cousin of Osceola...14
Cousins..13, 37
Creek Chief Red Shoes I..29
Creek metis...29
Creek Nation..13, 40
Creek War Claims...33
Cuff..36
customary...40
Damages...33
Dancing Rabbit Creek...17
Daphne...36
daughter of privilege...14
David Tate...13, 20
Delia..42
Delphine...40
deponent's...21
descendants...44

SOURCES

disappearance *20*
discrimination *44*
dissatisfied *44*
dissident *20*
dividends *37*
Doak's Stand *17*
Dolives *27*
Dreisbach *26*
East Florida *18, 23*
Elijah *27*
Elijah Tarvin *30*
Elise Moniac *29*
Elisha Tarvin *30*
Elizabeth [Elijah] Tarvin *30*
Elizabeth [Isabel Nash] *27*
Elouise [Eloisa] Tunstall *30*
English *23*
enumerated *25, 39*
escaped *20*
EuroIndian *40*
Excerpted *36*
expansion, as promised by their elected officials. ... *23*
Feliciana *21*
female relative *40*
Final Settlement *43*
Five Civilized Tribes *14*
Flora *29, 36, 40*
Floridians *23*
forfeiture *44*
Fort Adams *17*
Fort Charlotte *40*
Fort Mims *20*
Fort St. Stephens *17*
Fredonia *27*
Free *34*
friendly *39*
Frontier Claims in the Lower South *25*

SOURCES

General..*19, 23*
Genoveva..*27*
George Matthews..*23*
George Stiggins..*13*
Georgia...*23*
Georgians...*18*
gin..*32*
Grassroots of America...*28*
Great Britain..*23*
Guardianship...*37*
Hannah..*40*
Hardy...*36*
Harry..*35p.*
heirs...*39*
Hoe Buckintoopa...*17*
hostilities...*39*
House of Representatives..*38*
hundreds..*20*
indemnification..*39*
Indemnity...*33*
Indian descent...*20*
Indians...*39*
intermarriage...*40*
interrogatories...*40*
intrigue..*18*
invaded..*18, 23*
invasion...*23*
inventory..*35*
Isaacs...*29*
Jack..*40*
James..*19, 27*
James D. Dreisbach...*40*
James Thomas..*21*
Jeanette..*29*
Jefferson..*18*
John...*27*
John Randon...*20, 43*

SOURCES

John Weatherford 27
Johnston 27
Jonah 36
Joseph Booth 37
Joseph Stiggins 13
Josephine Bonaparte Tate [Dreisbach] 31
Josephine Bonarparte 20
Josephine Tate 30
Joyce 27
Judge Henry Johnson 21
justice of the peace 14
Lachlin McGillivray 29
Land Holdings 28
language 40
Last Will and Testament 36
Latchlin 29
Lee Slaughter 37
Little Warrior 19
Louis Marchand de Cortel 29
Louise 36
Louisiana, ... 21
Lucinda 42
Madison 23
Madison administration 23
Malcolm McPherson 29
manumission 21
Margaret Dyer 13
Margaret Dyer-Powell 13, 31
Margaret Tate 13
Maria 36
Maria Josephina Juzan 39
Mariah 42
Marsalina 27
Martha 14, 40
Martha [Polly] Dyer 26
Martha Ann Bryant [Crow] 27
Martha Bates 38

SOURCES

Mary Cussins *13, 26*
Mary Delphine *14*
Mary Dyer *13*
Mary Hollinger *39*
Mary Louise Randon *20*
Mary Randon *14*
Mary Sizemore *38*
massacre *20*
Massacre at Fort Mimms, 1813 .... *25*
McGillivray *29*
McIntosh Bluff *38*
McIntosh's Bluff *27*
member of Congress *21*
Milfort *29*
Mims *19*
Mississippi *17*
Mississippi Territory *38*
Mixed-Bloods *15*
Mobile *18, 33, 40*
Monday *42*
Moniac *26*
Montpelier *34*
Mount Dexter *17*
Natchez District *17*
Natchez Trace *17*
Natchez-Choctaw *13*
Native Americans *22*
Ned *35*
Negroes *37*
neighbors *40*
neutrality *33*
Nomathle Emautla *29*
North Carolina *18*
Nuncupative *30*
Old Joe *36*
only daughter *20*
Patriot War *23*

SOURCES

patriots ... *18*
Patriots ... *23*
Patsy [Martha] Dyer ... *38*
Pearl ... *28*
Peg ... *35*
Peggy Bailey ... *38*
Penny Coleman ... *40*
petitioned ... *38, 44*
Phoebe ... *36*
Pierre Juzan ... *43*
plantation ... *20*
policy ... *22*
Polly ... *40*
Polly Coleman ... *14*
predeceased ... *21*
Purchase ... *32*
Randon ... *27*
Red Eagle ... *22*
Red Shoes II ... *29*
Red Stick ... *19p.*
region ... *18*
relic ... *37*
Removal ... *17, 22*
Removal of 1830 ... *22*
renegade ... *19*
representative ... *21*
reservations ... *39*
reservee ... *44*
residence ... *44*
residents ... *23*
Reuben ... *40*
Reuben [Nathan] Dyer ... *37*
Reuben Dyer ... *13, 25*
Richard Coleman ... *28*
Richard Cussins ... *13*
rubric seal ... *37*
Sam ... *40*

SOURCES

Samuel Mims *20*
Scots trader *29*
securities *37*
Sehoy I. *29*
seize *18*
Seller *40*
Seminole War *20*
settlers *18, 23*
Sickey *36*
slave concubine *43*
slave revolt *20*
slaveholder *43*
slaves *14, 20*
Sophia *29*
Southern *18*
Spanish authorities *23*
Spanish land grant *38*
Spanish Land Grant *27*
Spanish occupancy *28*
St. Augustine *23*
Staples *26*
Stratford *42*
surnames *15*
Tecumseh *33*
Tennessee *28*
Tensaw *18*
Tensaw/Tombigbee *18*
territory *18*
Thaddeus *42*
The attack on Fort Mimms *9*
Thelps *21*
Theophilus *40*
Theresa *30*
Theresa [Elisha] Tarvin *30*
Thomas *27, 42*
Thomas Atkinson *37*
Thomas G. Holmes *43*

SOURCES

Todd	43
Tombigbee Alabama River	17
Tombigbee River	13
transgenerational	22
Treaty of Fort Jackson	21
Treaty of the Hickory Ground	39
Tuckabatchee	29
Tunstall	30
Tura Dyer	20
Tura Dyer-Randon, and mother Mary Dyer	21
waiver	44
Wallace	43
war	18
War	19
War of 1812	20, 23
watershed	17
Weatherford	26, 40
Weatherford v. Weatherford, et al. trial	40
Webster	42
West Florida	23, 33
white privilege	21
Whitney	32
Widow Margaret Tate	30
wife	36
Wilkinson	19, 33
William	27, 36
William	14
William Brown	37
William C. Wade	21
William Collins	21
William Dixon Moniac	29
William Powell	38
William Theophilus	14
William Theophilus Powell	13, 20
William Weatherford	22, 29
witness	37
Zephaniah Kingsley	23

SOURCES

Creek Indian History..13
throughout the borderlands..18
[Nancy] Haw Grey Stiggins..13
[Tallasee] Hickory Ground..29

www.ingramcontent.com/pod-product-compliance
Lightning Source LLC
Chambersburg PA
CBHW021848220426
43663CB00005B/446